PRIEST, PROPHET & KING

Living Your Baptismal Mission in Everyday Life

Allan Smith

Copyright © 2025 Allan J. Smith

All rights reserved. No part of this book may be reproduced in any form without written permission from the publisher, except brief quotations used in reviews or articles.

Scripture quotations in this book are from the Revised Standard Version – Catholic Edition, Second Edition (RSV-2CE), copyright © 2006 by the Division of Christian Education of the National Council of the Churches of Christ in the United States of America. Used by permission. All rights reserved.

Excerpts from the works of Archbishop Fulton J. Sheen are used with permission where applicable.

Published by: Bishop Sheen Today
www.bishopsheentoday.com

Title: Priest, Prophet & King. Living Your Baptismal Mission in Everyday Life.

Compiled by Allan J. Smith. Includes bibliographical references.

Identifiers:

Paperback: 978-1-997931-19-5

eBook: 978-1-997931-18-8

Hardcover: 978-1-997931-17-1

Subjects: Jesus Christ — Priest – Prophet – King — Prayer and Meditation – Grace of Baptism – Archbishop Fulton J. Sheen – Lives of the Saints

iv

DEDICATION

To Our Lady of the Holy Name of God

&

To The Holy Souls in Purgatory

Ora Pro Nobis

EPIGRAPH

"The laity must realize that their baptism is an ordination to action, to sanctify the temporal order."
— ***Archbishop Fulton J. Sheen***

PREFACE

A Call to Mission

One evening at a men's conference, after a talk on the call to holiness, a father approached me with tears in his eyes.

He said, "I always thought being a good dad meant working hard and keeping food on the table. Tonight, I realized God is asking me to lead my family to heaven."

His words stayed with me because they capture the heart of this book: every baptized person — father, mother, single or married — is summoned to something far greater than mere survival.
We are called to a royal mission.

For years I have spoken in seminaries, parishes, and conferences across North America, encouraging seminarians to embrace the sacrificial heart of the priesthood and inviting families to see their homes as "little churches." Again and again, I encountered the same hunger: ordinary Catholics longing to know how their baptism makes them participants in Christ's own work.

Whether I was teaching future priests about the Holy Eucharist or addressing parents about raising children in the faith, the message was clear — God's people are eager to live their identity as priest, prophet, and king.

Why This Book

Baptism is more than a welcome ritual or a family tradition.

It is the moment when Christ claims us, anoints us, and sends us.

Yet many Christians quietly forget this royal dignity.

We settle for being passive spectators in the Church instead of active disciples.

This book is an invitation to reclaim the full meaning of our baptism.

As priests, we offer the sacrifices of our daily lives in union with Christ's sacrifice on the Cross.

As prophets, we speak the truth in love and hand on the faith to our children and our culture.

As kings, we lead by humble service, bringing the peace of Christ to our families and communities.

Invitation to the Reader

The pages ahead are arranged to guide you step by step:

- **Part I** (Chapters 1–3) uncovers our identity in Christ and the beautiful truth of the domestic church.
- **Part II** (Chapters 4–5) explores our priestly mission in family life and in fostering vocations.
- **Part III** (Chapters 6–7) invites you to the prophetic task of evangelization and teaching the faith.

- **Part IV** (Chapters 8–10) shows how Christ's kingship is exercised through servant leadership and building a household of peace.
- **Part V** (Chapters 11–14) offers practical pathways, prayer, and real-life guidance for living out your mission.

Read it slowly.

Pray with the Scriptures.

Let the Holy Spirit reveal the unique way He is calling you to live your baptismal mission.

Dedication & Blessing

I dedicate this work to every family striving to make their home a sanctuary of faith, to every seminarian discerning the priesthood, and to every lay disciple who longs to see Christ reign in the ordinary rhythms of life.

May the Lord who called you by name at your baptism renew your heart as you read these pages.

May He strengthen you to be priest, prophet, and king in your home, your parish, and the world — until His kingdom comes in glory.

Table of Contents

Preface: A Call to Mission vii

PART I
IDENTITY

Chapter 1: The Dignity of Baptism 1

Chapter 2: The Royal Anointing: Sharing in Christ's Threefold Mission 6

Chapter 3: The Domestic Church: Where Mission Begins 10

PART II
PRIESTLY MISSION

Chapter 4: The Priest at Home, Work, And World 15

Chapter 5: Fostering Vocations and Spiritual Fatherhood 21

PART III
PROPHETIC MISSION

Chapter 6: The Prophet in Family and Culture 26

Chapter 7: Mission in the Modern World 31

PART IV
KINGLY MISSION

Chapter 8: Ordering the Heart: Self-Mastery and Virtue 37

Chapter 9: Building a House of Peace and Justice 45

Chapter 10: Living the Kingly Mission in Daily Life 52

PART V
LIVING THE MISSION

Chapter 11: Prayer, Sacraments, And Spiritual Warfare 60

Chapter 12: The Works of Mercy 68

Chapter 13: Testimony, Witness & Evangelization 76

Chapter 14: The Christian Life as a Missionary Journey 85

Epilogue: A Lifestyle of Missionary Joy 93

CHAPTER 1

The Dignity of Baptism

Baptism is the doorway to the Christian life — the moment when heaven touches earth, grace pours into the soul, and a new identity is bestowed. Yet for many Catholics, baptism is remembered mainly through photos, family stories, or the white garment tucked away in a drawer. Few realize that this sacrament is the foundation of everything that follows: our vocation, our mission, our transformation in Christ.

To understand who we are, we must first understand what baptism makes us.

A New Identity in Christ

At baptism, God does far more than welcome us into the Church.

He claims us.

He speaks the same words over us that He spoke over His beloved Son:

"You are mine."

Baptism is:

- **Adoption into God's family**
- **The washing away of sin**
- **A new birth in the Spirit**
- **Entrance into the Body of Christ**
- **A share in Christ's threefold mission as priest, prophet, and king**

Through water and the Spirit, God plants His own divine life in our souls.

This new identity is not symbolic or merely emotional — it is ontological. Something real changes within us. We become new creations.

"See what love the Father has given us, that we should be called children of God; and so we are" (1 John 3:1).

The Royal Anointing

In the early Church, baptism was immediately followed by an anointing with sacred chrism. This wasn't a decorative ritual. The anointing signified that the newly baptized shared in the very mission of Christ Himself — as **priest**, **prophet**, and **king**.

This means:

- **Priest** — We offer our lives in spiritual sacrifice
- **Prophet** — We speak God's truth with love
- **King** — We lead with service, virtue, and justice

Every baptized person receives this triple dignity and responsibility. It is not reserved for priests or religious. It belongs to every Christian.

Your baptism was your ordination to mission.

A Share in Christ's Victory

Baptism also brings us into Christ's Paschal Mystery — His death and resurrection. St. Paul writes:

"We were buried therefore with him by baptism into death, so that as Christ was raised from the dead... we too might walk in newness of life" (Romans 6:4).

This means:

- The old self is crucified
- The new self is raised
- We are empowered to fight sin
- We are strengthened to live in grace

Baptism is not simply a past event — it is a living power.

We can return to its grace daily with confidence: *"I belong to Christ. His victory is mine."*

Belonging to the Body of Christ

To be baptized is to be grafted into a family — a communion that stretches across time and space. It means:

- We are no longer spiritual orphans
- We are united to the saints in heaven
- We share one faith, one hope, one baptism
- We belong to a mission larger than ourselves

This belonging brings responsibilities and blessings.

We support one another in prayer, charity, and sacrifice.

We are called to build up the Church with our gifts.

Baptism gives us a place, a purpose, and a people.

The Domestic Church Begins Here

The grace of baptism finds its first home in the family.

Parents become the "first heralds of the faith."

The Christian home becomes the first chapel, the first school of virtue, and the first place where the Gospel is lived.

Every family becomes, in a real sense, a small church — a domestic sanctuary where Christ dwells.

Living from Our Baptism

Baptism is not meant to fade into a memory.

It is a daily summons to:

- Pray with confidence
- Live with courage
- Serve with joy
- Love with Christ's own love
- Reject sin and resist evil
- Build the Kingdom of God in the ordinary world

To live from our baptism is to remember who we are:

Beloved children of the Father, united to Christ, filled with the Holy Spirit.

This chapter sets the foundation for everything that follows.

Before we can act as priest, prophet, and king, we must first know our dignity — the dignity bestowed by God at the moment of our baptism.

CHAPTER 2

The Royal Anointing: Sharing in Christ's Threefold Mission

At baptism, the Church places sacred chrism upon the head of the newly baptized and pronounces words that echo through a lifetime: *"As Christ was anointed Priest, Prophet, and King, so may you live always as a member of His body."*

This single moment defines the Christian vocation.

It tells us not only **who we are**, but **what we are called to become**.

Christ does not keep His mission for Himself.

He shares it.

And because we share His anointing, we also share His work.

Sharing in Christ's Priesthood

The priesthood of the baptized is not liturgical — that belongs to the ordained priest.

But every Christian shares in a *spiritual priesthood*, offering sacrifices pleasing to God.

This means:

- We offer our joys and sorrows
- We unite our work to Christ's work
- We sanctify daily life through prayer
- We intercede for others

A parent waking at night with a child, a worker enduring a difficult day, a caregiver tending to the sick — these become priestly acts when united to Christ's sacrifice.

Your life becomes an altar.

Sharing in Christ's Prophetic Mission

A prophet is one who hears God's Word and speaks it with love.

Through baptism, each of us is commissioned to:

- Announce the Gospel through our lives
- Speak truth in a world confused by falsehood
- Teach the faith to our children
- Encourage others in virtue
- Bear witness to hope

You do not need eloquence; you need fidelity.

God supplies the rest.

The world listens more to authenticity than to arguments.

A single honest word spoken with charity can open a heart.

Sharing in Christ's Kingship

Christ's kingship is not domination but service.

He reigns from the Cross, leading by love and self-gift.

Thus, our kingship is practiced whenever we:

- Govern ourselves with virtue
- Lead our families with humility
- Build peace in our homes
- Shape our surroundings with justice
- Steward our gifts for the good of others

Christian kingship begins with ruling one's own heart.

Only then can it extend outward with integrity.

The Three Missions Together

Priest, prophet, and king are not separate roles.

They interlock — each strengthening the other.

- **Priest** — you offer your life to God
- **Prophet** — you speak God's truth
- **King** — you lead with God's love

When lived together, these missions transform families, parishes, and communities.

A home where Christ's threefold mission is lived becomes a beacon of charity, truth, and peace.

A Daily Renewal

Baptism planted the seeds of these missions.

Daily faithfulness allows them to grow.

Practical daily renewal:

- Begin the day with the Sign of the Cross
- Offer your work and sacrifices
- Speak words of encouragement
- Guide others gently and wisely
- End each day with gratitude

These simple habits strengthen the royal anointing within you.

A Mission for Every Christian

This chapter reveals that the Christian mission is not reserved for a few.

Every baptized believer participates in Christ's saving work.

You have been:

- Anointed
- Empowered
- Sent

The rest of the book will show how this mission takes shape in the home, the parish, and the world.

CHAPTER 3

The Domestic Church: Where Mission Begins

The Christian home is not merely a private residence.

It is the first chapel, the first school, and the first community where faith is taught, nurtured, and lived. Long before a child hears a homily or learns a catechism lesson, the home has already formed the heart.

This is why the Church calls the family the **"domestic church."**

It is here that the baptismal mission of priest, prophet, and king first takes root in daily life.

Your home is holy ground.

The Family as a Living Sanctuary

Every Christian family — regardless of size, structure, or circumstance — is called to reflect the presence of Christ. Not through perfection, but through fidelity.

A domestic church:

- Prays together
- Lives forgiveness

- Practices charity
- Welcomes others
- Keeps Christ at the center

A family does not need to be ideal to be holy. It needs only to open its doors to grace.

Holiness begins in ordinary rhythms: meals shared, prayers whispered, burdens carried together.

Parents as First Evangelizers

Before any priest, teacher, or parish minister has the chance to speak, parents have already preached countless sermons through:

- Their example
- Their patience
- Their words of encouragement
- Their way of loving and listening

Children learn the faith primarily by watching it lived.

A mother kneeling in prayer, a father blessing a child before bed, a family faithfully attending Mass — these become seeds that grow for a lifetime.

You do not need theological degrees to teach the faith.

You need faithfulness.

The Home as the First School of Prayer

Prayer does not begin in the sanctuary of a church.

It begins in the sanctuary of the home.

Simple practices can turn a family dwelling into an oasis of grace:

- Morning offering
- Grace before meals
- Nightly blessings
- Liturgical candles in Advent
- A small prayer corner
- Scripture read aloud

What matters most is consistency and love.

When a child sees prayer woven naturally into family life, faith becomes not an obligation but a way of being.

The Domestic Church as a School of Virtue

Families learn virtue not by lectures but by practice:

- Patience when tempers rise
- Forgiveness after conflict
- Humility in admitting mistakes
- Gratitude at the table
- Generosity toward those in need

Each moment of trial becomes an opportunity to shape the heart in virtue.

A holy home is not one without disagreements, but one where mercy always has the last word.

Hospitality as Evangelization

A home that welcomes becomes a place of evangelization.

Hospitality does not require spotless floors or perfect meals. It requires presence and love.

When families open their homes for meals, fellowship, or simple companionship, they create space for grace to work quietly and powerfully.

Many conversions begin not in the pews, but at kitchen tables.

Suffering in the Domestic Church

Every family carries wounds and struggles: illness, financial strain, misunderstandings, aging parents, wandering children. These difficulties do not disqualify a family from holiness.

They sanctify it.

When families unite their trials to Christ, their home becomes a place of redemptive love. Children who witness faith in suffering learn a profound lesson:

God is faithful even in the storm.

A Mission Rooted in Love

The domestic church is the primary arena where the baptismal missions are lived:

- **Priest:** offering daily sacrifices
- **Prophet:** proclaiming the truth with love
- **King:** leading by service and peace

Strong families form strong parishes.

Strong parishes form strong communities.

Strong communities transform culture.

This is where mission begins — not in distant lands, but in living rooms, kitchens, and family prayer corners.

CHAPTER 4

The Priest at Home, Work, and World

Living the Daily Offering of Baptized Priesthood

Every baptized Christian shares in the priesthood of Christ — not the ministerial priesthood of the altar, but the **common priesthood of the faithful**, expressed through sacrifice, prayer, and love.

While ordained priests offer the Eucharistic Sacrifice in persona Christi, the baptized offer their lives **in communion with that sacrifice**, turning daily duties into holy offerings.

This chapter explores how ordinary Christians live their priestly mission in the three primary spheres of life: **home**, **work**, and **the world**.

1. The Priest in the Home

The home is the first place where the priestly mission takes shape.

Every Christian — married, single, parent, grandparent — is called to **sanctify daily life** through prayer and self-giving love.

Daily Sacrifice

The priestly heart learns to see:

- Changing diapers
- Cleaning the kitchen
- Rising early for work
- Caring for aging parents
- Bearing illness with faith

as **offerings placed on the altar of life**.

When united to the Eucharist, small sacrifices become holy acts that sanctify the family.

Intercessory Prayer

A priestly home is one where intercession rises like incense. Pray for:

- Spouses
- Children
- Relatives
- Friends
- The suffering
- The lukewarm
- The wandering

These hidden prayers carry enormous spiritual power.

A family that prays together forms a fortress of grace.

Sanctifying the Rhythms of Family Life

Simple practices help make the home a sanctuary:

- Bless your family members
- Celebrate baptismal anniversaries
- Read Scripture aloud
- Pray before meals
- Offer a nightly prayer of forgiveness

Such rhythms lift the home toward heaven.

2. The Priest at Work

The workplace is often the largest mission field a Christian will ever enter.

Most people will never read a theology book, but they will read **your life**.

Work as Offering

Every task — whether manual labor, teaching, business leadership, or hidden administrative work — becomes a priestly act when offered to God.

Start the day with:

"Lord, I offer this work to You for the glory of Your name and the good of those I serve."

This transforms routine into worship.

Integrity as Witness

Priestly witness in the workplace includes:
- Honesty in words and actions
- Refusing gossip
- Speaking truth with charity
- Treating coworkers with dignity
- Working with diligence and humility

Integrity evangelizes without words.

Carrying Christ into Daily Encounters

A priestly presence at work brings:
- Peace where there is tension
- Encouragement where there is discouragement
- Patience where there is frustration
- Listening where no one else listens

You may be the only image of Christ your coworkers ever encounter.

3. The Priest in the World

Beyond home and work lies the broader arena of cultural, civic, and social life.

Offering the World to God

Christians consecrate the world through:

- Presence
- Prayer
- Compassion
- Beauty
- Moral courage

The baptized priest stands in the midst of the world, holding it before God in intercession.

Acting as a Bridge

A priest is a bridge.

A Christian becomes a bridge wherever he or she:

- Reconciles friends who are divided
- Brings peace into conflict
- Serves the poor
- Offers forgiveness
- Defends the dignity of human life

Such actions transform ordinary settings into places of grace.

Living the Eucharist Beyond the Mass

The dismissal at Mass — *"Go forth"* — is not a polite conclusion. It is a commissioning.

We carry Christ:

- Into neighborhoods
- Grocery stores
- Hospitals
- Social gatherings
- Volunteer service
- Public life

The Eucharist becomes visible through our charity.

A Life Poured Out

The essence of priesthood — ordained or baptismal — is self-offering.

A life poured out in love becomes a chalice lifted to God.

Wherever you stand today — in the kitchen, the office, the classroom, the checkout line — Christ invites you to unite your heart to His sacrifice. Nothing is too small to become holy when offered with love.

CHAPTER 5

Fostering Vocations and Spiritual Fatherhood

The Seedbed of Every Vocation

Every vocation begins where Christ first takes root — in the home. Long before a young man enters seminary or a young woman begins discerning religious life, their hearts are shaped by the quiet fidelity, sacrifice, and love they see lived around them. The Church has long taught that *the family is the first seminary*, the place where faith becomes flesh in the daily rhythm of life.

Children learn to pray not from textbooks, but from parents who pray.

They learn to love the Mass from families who worship faithfully.

They learn generosity from fathers and mothers who give of themselves day after day.

No bishop, pastor, or vocation director can replace the witness of a holy home.

A vocation is not "produced." It is awakened — nurtured by a family that sees God's will as the greatest treasure a child could discover.

Spiritual Fatherhood: A Priestly Role

Every baptized man shares in Christ's priestly mission.

This does not diminish the ministerial priesthood — it supports it.

The common priesthood of the faithful is meant to create fertile soil where ordained vocations can flourish.

A father exercises spiritual fatherhood when he:

- Leads his family in prayer
- Blesses his children
- Confesses his sins humbly
- Provides through sacrifice
- Protects the spiritual atmosphere of the home
- Discerns with his spouse how to guide each child toward holiness

Spiritual fatherhood is not about authority; it is about availability.

It is about a man who stands in the breach for his family, who radiates the love of Christ the High Priest through his patience, devotion, and integrity.

When a child has seen authentic fatherhood, a priest's fatherhood becomes intelligible and attractive.

Encouraging Vocations in the Parish and Community

Fostering vocations is never merely a private task — it is a mission shared by the entire Christian community.

A parish that takes vocations seriously:

- Prays regularly for seminarians and religious
- Celebrates ordinations, professions, and anniversaries
- Invites priests and religious to share their vocation stories
- Offers youth opportunities for service, Eucharistic adoration, and mission
- Creates an atmosphere where the call of God is normal, beautiful, and expected

When a parish honors the priesthood, children learn to love it.

When families speak positively of priests, they sustain them.

When the community surrounds young people who are discerning, they give courage for the next step.

A vocation is not a private possession — it is a gift to the whole Church.

Practical Pathways for Families

Here are simple, concrete ways to cultivate a vocation-friendly home:

- Keep a family prayer routine, even if brief
- Bring children regularly before the Blessed Sacrament
- Celebrate baptismal anniversaries
- Read short lives of the saints together
- Encourage Christian service as a normal part of life
- Speak reverently of priests and religious
- Ask your children occasionally:
  "What do you think God might be calling you to?"
- Show joy in your own vocation — married or single

The question is not whether God is calling young people.

He always is.

The question is whether the environment is quiet enough, joyful enough, faithful enough for them to hear Him.

Closing Reflection

The priesthood, religious life, and holy marriages do not arise in a vacuum—they spring from homes where Christ is loved.

Fostering vocations begins when families embrace their priestly identity and men step into the noble task of spiritual fatherhood. Every father, by his faithfulness, becomes a living icon of God the Father. Every mother, by her tenderness and courage, prepares the soil where a child can hear the whisper of God.

To foster vocations is simply to create a home where holiness is natural, sacrifice is honored, and God's will is desired above everything else.

Reflection Questions

1. How can I strengthen the spiritual atmosphere of my home?
2. Do my children see joy in my own vocation?

How can I support vocations in my parish or community today?

CHAPTER 6

The Prophet in Family and Culture

Christ the Prophet and the Baptized

Jesus Christ is the Eternal Word of the Father — the Prophet promised to Moses, the One who speaks truth not as a messenger but as Truth Himself. When we are baptized, we receive a share in this prophetic identity.

A prophet is not simply someone who predicts the future.

A prophet reveals God's presence in the present moment.

To be prophetic means:

- To listen to God
- To speak with clarity
- To witness with one's life
- To make God visible where He seems forgotten

The world does not need more noise. It needs more witnesses.

As Archbishop Sheen said:

> **"Truth without love is brutality;
> love without truth is sentimentality."**

Prophets hold both together.

Every Christian is called to speak truth in love — beginning at home and extending outward into society.

Forming a Prophetic Home

The family is the first school of truth.

Before any child learns doctrine, they learn sincerity, virtue, and integrity by observing the adults around them.

A prophetic home is not perfect.

It is honest.

It is the place where children discover:

- That truth matters
- That words must match actions
- That forgiveness is possible
- That God's Word guides our decisions

Parents become the first prophets in their children's lives when they:

- Read Scripture aloud
- Bring the family to Mass faithfully

- Speak reverently of the Church and her teachings
- Teach the meaning of right and wrong
- Discern decisions in the light of the Gospel
- Share their faith naturally at the dinner table, in the car, or before bed

A prophetic home is formed not by dramatic gestures but by steady, faithful witness.

When a home is anchored in truth, it becomes a small lighthouse in a drifting world.

Speaking the Truth in a Confused Culture

Today's culture is noisy, distracted, and often hostile to Christian belief. Yet this is precisely where the prophetic voice of the baptized is needed.

Prophetic witness is not about conquering arguments; it is about revealing Christ's presence.

You live your prophetic mission when you:

- Stand for the dignity of life
- Defend marriage with clarity and compassion
- Refuse to participate in gossip or slander
- Choose honesty in business
- Encourage virtue in your children
- Speak calmly when others speak with anger
- Practice forgiveness when the world demands vengeance

Prophets are bridge-builders, not bomb-throwers.

They shine light without shaming, and they correct without condemning.

To live prophetically is to live visibly Christian — not ostentatiously, but unmistakably.

The world may resist the truth, but it cannot ignore a life transformed by it.

Living Prophecy with Courage and Charity

Every prophetic mission requires courage.

Jeremiah felt fear.

Ezekiel felt inadequacy.

Even Moses hesitated before God.

God does not call the powerful;

He empowers the called.

Prophetic courage is found in:

- Daily prayer
- Frequent reception of the sacraments
- Fidelity to Scripture
- Quiet acts of charity
- The support of a Christian community

Charity is the prophetic heart.

Courage is the prophetic backbone.

When the baptized combine both, they become instruments of grace in their families, workplaces, and parishes.

Holiness speaks.

Joy evangelizes.

Sacrifice converts.

Closing Reflection

To be a prophet is to let God speak through your life.

You do not need a stage, a microphone, or an audience.

You need only a heart willing to listen and a life willing to obey.

Your family becomes prophetic when it lives the Gospel openly.

Your parish becomes prophetic when charity and clarity meet.

Your culture is evangelized one honest word and one faithful life at a time.

Reflection Questions

1. Where is God inviting me to speak truth with greater courage?
2. How can my home become a place where Scripture, virtue, and honesty flourish?

What small prophetic act can I make today in my family, workplace, or parish?

CHAPTER 7

Mission in the Modern World

The World as Mission Territory

The world our Lord sends us into is not the same world the apostles walked — yet the human heart remains unchanged.

People still hunger for truth, belonging, mercy, forgiveness, and hope.

Every age has its particular challenges.

Ours is marked by:

- Secularism
- Distraction
- Loneliness
- Moral confusion
- Technological overload
- Deep suspicion of institutional religion

Yet these very conditions make the modern world ripe for mission.

As Fulton Sheen once said:

"The human heart is always the same.
Scratch beneath the surface of any age,
and you will find the same longing for God."

Your mission field is not somewhere "out there."

It is the very world you inhabit:

- Your neighborhood
- Your workplace
- Your parish
- Your friendships
- Your online presence
- Your family gatherings

Evangelization today is not about escaping culture, but illuminating it with the light of Christ.

Living Faith Publicly

In a world that prizes privacy and warns believers to "keep religion to yourself," the Christian must rediscover the gentle courage of public witness.

Public witness does not mean grand speeches or heated debates. It means quiet faithfulness:

- Making the Sign of the Cross before meals
- Keeping Sunday holy

- Wearing sacramentals naturally
- Speaking well of the Church
- Rejecting gossip and negativity
- Refusing to compromise moral truths
- Offering to pray for someone in need

When faith becomes visible, it becomes invitational.

Modern mission begins when Christians stop hiding the light they carry.

The world is not offended by holiness — it is starved for it.

Digital Discipleship & Modern Arenas

Never in history has the average person had such power to influence others.

One post can reach thousands.

A short message can comfort a stranger.

A simple act of kindness online can counter a tide of negativity.

The digital realm is a real mission field.

Yet it requires discernment.

A Christian is a disciple even behind a keyboard.

We evangelize in the digital world when we:

- Share uplifting content
- Speak respectfully, even in disagreement
- Avoid sarcasm, cruelty, and mockery

- Refuse to spread misinformation
- Offer hope, encouragement, and truth
- Share Scripture and testimonies appropriately
- Protect our hearts with healthy limits

St. Paul wrote letters.

Today we write posts, comments, replies, and emails.

The same Holy Spirit who guided him desires to guide us.

Your online presence may introduce Christ to people you will never meet in person.

Navigating Cultural Challenges with Truth & Charity

Modern society often demands conformity rather than truth.

It praises self-invention, rejects objective morality, and treats faith as an outdated relic.

The Christian response must be neither retreat nor aggression, but **charity rooted in clarity**.

A missionary disciple today must learn the art of:

- Listening before speaking
- Disagreeing without hostility
- Explaining without attacking
- Affirming the dignity of every person
- Holding firm to Catholic teaching without compromise

Truth without love alienates.

Love without truth deceives.

Prophetic mission insists on both.

When a Christian speaks with peace, confidence, and compassion, the world takes notice — even when it disagrees.

Hope as a Missionary Witness

The greatest evangelization tool in the modern age is not argument but **hope**.

People today are discouraged:

- Families are fragmented
- Violence fills the news
- Anxiety and depression rise
- Faith seems to be fading
- Many feel spiritually orphaned

A hopeful Christian stands out.

A peaceful heart in a restless culture is a sign of contradiction.

Your hope is a beacon:

- When you trust God in difficulty
- When you remain joyful in trial
- When you speak confidently of God's providence
- When you radiate peace amid uncertainty

Hope is the missionary virtue the world is starving for.

As Sheen said:

> "The world is full of half-truths;
> it hungers for a whole hope."

Closing Reflection

To live mission in the modern world is to let Christ shine through you — in your speech, your habits, your decisions, and your joy. The Church does not fear the modern age; she is sent into it.

Your life becomes a missionary witness each time you choose truth, charity, and hope in a world that often chooses the opposite.

Reflection Questions

1. Where is God inviting me to be more visibly Christian in my daily life?

2. How can I use the digital world for evangelization rather than distraction?

3. What opportunities exist in my own culture, workplace, or neighborhood for gentle witness?

Do I radiate hope in a way that draws others to Christ?

CHAPTER 8

Ordering the Heart: Self-Mastery and Virtue

Introduction — The Kingly Mission Begins Within

Before a Christian can bring order, justice, and peace to the world, he must first allow Christ to establish order in his own heart.

The kingly mission of the baptized is not primarily about governing others — it is about governing oneself.

Fulton Sheen often taught:

> "The greatest empire to rule is the empire within."

Virtue is the training ground of kingship.

Without it, the Christian becomes divided, enslaved by impulses, or swept along by the culture.

With it, the Christian becomes free, courageous, and capable of genuine love.

This chapter explores how to cultivate the interior freedom and self-mastery that allow Christ to reign within us — so that His peace may radiate outward into our families, parishes, and the world.

I. The Call to Interior Order

God is a God of order, harmony, and peace.

Sin introduces disorder — thoughts scattered, desires conflicted, choices weakened.

Grace comes to restore what sin has disrupted.

The Christian life is a lifelong journey of interior alignment:

- **Mind** renewed by truth
- **Will** strengthened by grace
- **Passions** ordered toward charity
- **Habits** shaped by virtue

Self-mastery is not a matter of self-reliance but cooperation with grace.

We do not rearrange our inner world alone; Christ the King takes His throne within us, restoring peace one decision at a time.

Signs of an ordered heart:

- A growing sense of peace
- Increased patience in trial
- Clarity when discerning God's will
- Freedom from compulsions

- Greater capacity to love

An ordered heart becomes the foundation for everything else in the Christian mission.

II. The Virtues: Pathways to Freedom

Virtue is the steady power to choose the good with joy.

It is the true strength of a Christian king.

The Church identifies four **cardinal virtues** — the hinges upon which the moral life turns:

1. Prudence — Seeing Clearly

Prudence helps us discern the right course of action in each circumstance.

It is not hesitation but clarity — the ability to see as God sees.

Practical invitations:

- Pray before decisions, even small ones
- Seek counsel from wise, holy people
- Reflect on choices after the fact

2. Justice — Giving Each Their Due

Justice orders our relationships.

It makes us faithful in promises, respectful of others, and compassionate toward the vulnerable.

It is the virtue needed most urgently in a divided world.

3. Fortitude — Courage in Trial

Fortitude strengthens us to endure hardship and resist temptation.

It enables parents to persevere, priests to sacrifice, and disciples to remain faithful in struggle.

Courage grows every time we choose faith over fear.

4. Temperance — Mastery of Desire

Temperance frees us from being ruled by appetites.

It touches food, drink, entertainment, speech, sexuality, and all the passions.

A temperate person is not rigid but free — able to enjoy God's gifts without being enslaved by them.

III. Battling Interior Enemies

Every king must protect his kingdom.

So too the Christian must guard the heart.

The main adversaries are ancient and familiar:

- **Distraction**
- **Discouragement**
- **Anger**
- **Fear**
- **Sloth**
- **Disordered attachments**

- **Sinful habits**

These forces seek to weaken the soul's defenses.

Spiritual strategies for interior battle:

Daily examination of conscience
Helps recognize patterns and uproot sin early.

Frequent Confession
A sacrament not only of forgiveness but of strengthening.

Scripture meditation
Truth displaces lies and clarifies desires.

Fasting
Trains the will and opens space for grace.

Accountability
Inviting another believer to walk with you in holiness provides support and humility.

Self-mastery grows through small victories repeated over time.

IV. Christ the King: The Model of Interior Freedom

Jesus is the perfect image of ordered humanity.

His passions were fully obedient to the Father's will; His heart was at peace even in suffering.

The Gospels portray Him as:

- Calm amid storms
- Silent before false accusations
- Compassionate toward sinners

- Decisive when confronting evil
- Prayerful before every major decision

To imitate Christ is to allow His dispositions to take root in our soul.

As Sheen wrote:

> **"Christ did not come to make us nice;
> He came to make us new."**

Interior renewal is the crown of the kingly mission.

V. Bringing Peace to the Household

A heart ordered by grace becomes a source of peace for others.

Self-mastery equips the Christian to:

- Respond gently rather than react harshly
- Create a home atmosphere marked by patience and joy
- Lead children with calm, consistent love
- Diffuse conflict with humility
- Model forgiveness and reconciliation
- Make decisions that reflect God's wisdom

The home becomes a small kingdom where Christ reigns.

People naturally follow someone whose peace is steady, whose judgment is fair, and whose love remains firm.

This is the quiet strength of the Christian king.

VI. Practical Steps for Daily Growth

1. Begin each day with surrender.
"Jesus, reign in my heart today."

2. Choose one virtue to practice intentionally this week.

3. Create small habits of order:

- Make the bed
- Keep a tidy prayer space
- Maintain a simple schedule
- Limit unnecessary noise

Outer order supports inner order.

4. Fast once a week from something that distracts you.

5. End the day with gratitude and examination.

Holiness grows through humble, steady practice.

Reflection Questions

1. Which areas of my interior life feel most disordered or restless?
2. Which virtue is Christ inviting me to cultivate right now?
3. How might greater self-mastery transform my home environment?

Closing Prayer

Lord Jesus,
King of my heart,
establish Your peace within me.
Order my thoughts, govern my desires,
and strengthen my will by Your grace.
Make me faithful in virtue,
wise in decisions,
and gentle in all my dealings.
Reign in me, that I may bring Your peace
to my family, my parish, and my world.

Amen.

CHAPTER 9

Building a House of Peace and Justice

Introduction — The Kingdom Begins at Home

Every home is meant to be a small kingdom under the reign of Christ.

Peace does not begin in governments or institutions — it begins at the kitchen table, in the quiet interactions between spouses, in the way children are formed, and in the unspoken habits of love cultivated day after day.

Christ's kingship grows wherever His peace is chosen, practiced, defended, and shared.

Fulton Sheen often reminded families:

> "The home is the first and most important school of Christian living."

A peaceful household is not accidental; it is built, protected, and renewed through intentional, grace-filled choices.

This chapter offers a path to cultivating a home where justice and mercy meet, where relationships flourish, and where Christ's reign becomes visible in the ordinary rhythms of life.

I. Peace as the Fruit of Right Relationship

Christian peace is not the absence of conflict but the presence of harmony rooted in truth and love.

It flows from right relationships:

- **With God**
- **Within ourselves**
- **With our family**
- **With our community and the world**

When sin disrupts these relationships, peace fades.

When grace restores them, peace returns.

Jesus is the Prince of Peace, and where He is welcomed, order follows.

Three pillars of Christian peace:

1. **Truth** — honesty and clarity in conversations.
2. **Charity** — the willingness to seek another's good above our own.
3. **Mercy** — forgiveness that frees the heart and restores unity.

A household built on these three pillars stands firm even in trial.

II. Justice in the Christian Home

Justice is the virtue that gives each person their due — not according to worldly metrics but according to the dignity God has bestowed upon them.

In the home, justice looks like:

- **Respect** between spouses
- **Fairness** in duties and expectations
- **Honesty** in speech
- **Reliability** in promises
- **Honoring** the needs of the vulnerable (children, elderly parents, those burdened by sorrow)

Justice ensures that love is not sentimental but strong, steady, and real.

A just home is a healthy home.

III. Healing Family Wounds

No family is without tension, wounds, or misunderstandings.

The presence of conflict does not mean a home has failed; it means the family is human.

What matters is how we respond.

Forgiveness: the royal remedy

Forgiveness is the greatest work of a Christian king or queen. It is the sign that Christ truly reigns within the heart.

Forgiveness does **not** deny the wound; it chooses freedom over resentment.

Grace strengthens us to:

- Stop rehearsing old hurts
- Release grudges
- Pray for those who have wronged us
- Seek reconciliation in humility
- Apologize without excuses

Families flourish when forgiveness becomes a habit instead of a rare event.

IV. Communication That Builds, Not Breaks

Words create the emotional climate of a home.

Scripture reminds us:

> **"Death and life are in the power of the tongue."**
> — Proverbs 18:21

Healthy communication includes:

- Speaking truth in love
- Listening without defensiveness
- Avoiding sarcasm and unnecessary criticism
- Clarifying misunderstandings gently
- Addressing problems directly, not through passive aggression

A peaceful home is built on conversations that heal rather than harm.

V. Creating a Family Culture of Peace

Peace is not a feeling but a culture — one formed through repeated, intentional acts.

Practices that cultivate peace:

1. A prayerful home
Grace enters where prayer is welcome: a daily rosary, a short morning prayer, blessing meals, nighttime intercessions.

2. Order and routine
Regular meals, family responsibilities, and shared rhythms reduce stress and strengthen unity.

3. Celebrations of faith
Mark feast days, sacraments, birthdays, and anniversaries. Joy strengthens bonds.

4. Hospitality
Welcoming others into the home makes Christ's charity visible.

5. Sabbath rest
Keeping Sunday sacred brings God's rhythm into every week.

Peace grows where the Lord is honored.

VI. Justice Beyond the Home

A family formed in peace becomes a blessing to the world.

Christian households are meant to be:

- **Beacons of hope** in weary neighborhoods
- **Witnesses of stability** in a chaotic culture
- **Schools of charity** for the next generation

- **Sources of generosity** to the poor
- **Voices of truth** when society forgets God

Justice begins in the home but does not end there.

A family rooted in Christ becomes a force for good — quietly transforming workplaces, parishes, friendships, and communities.

VII. When Peace Falters: Starting Again

Even the holiest homes experience conflict, stress, and seasons of hardship.

The Christian response is not despair, but renewal.

When peace falters:

- Return to prayer
- Name the tension honestly
- Invite conversation, not blame
- Ask the Holy Spirit to soften hearts
- Recommit to forgiveness and charity

The family that keeps beginning again will never lose the path of holiness.

Grace rebuilds what we cannot.

Reflection Questions

1. What habits in my home promote peace?
2. Where does disorder or resentment hinder harmony?
3. What act of justice or forgiveness is Christ inviting me to take this week?

Closing Prayer

Lord Jesus, Prince of Peace,
enter our home and reign within our hearts.
Teach us to love with justice,
to forgive with mercy,
and to speak with truth and kindness.

Bless every room of our household,
every conversation, every decision.
Make our family a place of healing,
a refuge of peace,
and a small reflection of Your Kingdom.

Amen.

CHAPTER 10

Living the Kingly Mission in Daily Life

Introduction — Reigning Through Love

The kingship of Christ is unlike any earthly rule.

He reigns not by domination but by self-giving love.

To share in His kingly mission is to bring order, justice, and mercy into the ordinary moments of life — the small decisions, the daily habits, and the countless interactions that shape our character and influence those around us.

Every baptized Christian is called to be a steward of God's Kingdom in:

- the home,
- the workplace,
- the parish,
- and the wider community.

This chapter shows how to live Christ's kingship with humility and courage, allowing His peace and power to radiate through our everyday choices.

I. The Heart as the First Territory of Christ's Kingdom

Before a Christian can bring order to the world, they must let Christ bring order to their own heart.

Interior governance

Kingly leadership begins with self-mastery:

- governing emotions through grace
- resisting sinful impulses
- cultivating virtue
- committing to prayer
- keeping priorities aligned with God's will

A person who cannot govern themselves cannot govern anything else in a Christian spirit.

As Archbishop Fulton Sheen reminds us:

> **"The higher the structure, the deeper must be the foundation."**

Self-governance is the foundation upon which all Christian leadership rests.

II. Living Christ's Kingship in Family Life

The home is the primary place where the kingly mission becomes visible.

Leadership Through Service

Parents, especially fathers, exercise a beautiful kingship not by control but by sacrificial love:

- protecting the peace of the home
- setting spiritual priorities
- modeling virtues
- creating an atmosphere of respect
- placing the needs of others before their own

This is not authoritarian leadership — it is Christ-like leadership.

Cultivating Order and Purpose

A home ruled by love has:

- clear expectations
- shared responsibilities
- regular prayer
- a rhythm of work and rest
- space for joy, conversation, and creativity

When order governs external life, peace governs internal life.

III. Witnessing Christ's Kingship in the Workplace

The workplace is often the largest mission field for lay Catholics.

Christ's kingship appears in daily work when we:
- strive for excellence
- practice integrity
- avoid gossip and dishonesty
- honor coworkers with dignity
- speak truth with courage
- serve others without seeking credit

Holiness in the workplace is not about religious slogans — it is about living virtue under pressure.

Carrying Christ into secular settings

The Christian does not need to preach in the office; the radiance of patience, joy, and justice will do the preaching.

A calm spirit amid tension, a humble correction, or a consistent work ethic becomes a silent proclamation of the Kingdom.

IV. Building Communities of Peace and Accountability

Christians are called to shape their environments, not surrender to them.

Parish Life

Every parish needs:

- humble servants
- generous volunteers
- dependable leaders
- intercessors
- encouragers
- those who build bridges and heal divisions

Kingly mission in a parish means helping the community reflect Christ's unity and peace.

Broader Community

The Christian may not change the whole world, but they can change the corner of the world entrusted to them:

- neighborly kindness
- mentoring youth
- supporting the vulnerable
- advocating for justice
- showing up where others withdraw

Even simple acts — a meal delivered, a driveway cleared, a sincere conversation — extend Christ's reign.

V. Exercising Courage and Moral Clarity

The kingly mission includes standing firm in truth, especially when it is unpopular.

Courage rooted in charity

Christian courage is not loud or aggressive.

It is steady, peaceful, and motivated by love.

Courage appears when we:

- defend the dignity of life
- uphold marriage and family
- refuse to compromise integrity
- challenge corruption gently but firmly
- speak truth without bitterness

Christ the King reigns through hearts that refuse to bow to fear.

VI. Stewardship: Governing Resources for God's Glory

The kingly mission includes responsible stewardship over:

- time
- money
- talents
- opportunities
- relationships

Stewardship transforms ordinary management into holy service.

Time

Christians make time serve their salvation, not sabotage it.

Treasure

Generosity is the hallmark of a Christian king — freely sharing what God has freely given.

Talent

Every gift is a tool for building the Kingdom, not a trophy for display.

VII. The Cross: The Throne of Christian Kingship

Christ revealed His kingship most powerfully on the Cross.

There, love conquered sin; humility conquered pride; obedience conquered rebellion.

To share in His kingship is to share in His Cross:

- bearing suffering with patience
- offering trials for the salvation of souls
- forgiving those who wound us
- remaining faithful when discouraged

The Cross is where Christian authority is purified and perfected.

Reflection Questions

1. In which area of my life do I most need Christ to reign more fully?
2. How can I practice servant leadership in my family this week?
3. What small act of courage or integrity can I take in my workplace or community?

Closing Prayer

Lord Jesus Christ,
King of Heaven and Earth,
reign in my heart and in every corner of my life.

Teach me to govern myself with wisdom,
to lead my family with love,
to serve my community with justice,
and to walk each day with courage.

May Your Cross be my strength,
Your Spirit be my guide,
and Your Kingdom be my desire,
now and forever.

Amen.

CHAPTER 11

Prayer, Sacraments, and Spiritual Warfare

Introduction — Strength for the Journey

Every Christian vocation draws its power from intimacy with God.

Without prayer, the spiritual life withers. Without the sacraments, grace grows thin. Without vigilance, the enemy exploits every weakness.

Christians do not walk through a neutral world. We walk through a battlefield — but one in which Christ has already won the decisive victory.

Our task is not to defeat the devil but to **remain united to the One who has**.

This chapter explores how the baptized exercise their priestly, prophetic, and kingly identity by staying rooted in prayer, strengthened by sacrament, and alert in the spiritual struggle.

I. Prayer: Living in Relationship With God

Prayer is not a technique but a relationship.

It is the continual turning of the heart toward the One who loves us.

Daily prayer builds spiritual resilience

Just as the body weakens without food, the soul weakens without prayer.

A few simple commitments help anchor the day:

- **Morning offering** — giving the day to God
- **Short aspirations** — "Jesus, I trust in You"
- **Scripture meditation** — letting God speak
- **Examination of conscience** — asking for mercy and growth
- **Night prayer** — ending the day in peace

Small, steady habits produce profound inner strength.

Silence as a spiritual weapon

Silence is not the absence of noise but the presence of God.

In silence, the Holy Spirit reveals truth, heals wounds, and strengthens the will.

A noisy life leads to spiritual confusion.

A prayerful life leads to spiritual clarity.

II. The Sacraments: Wellsprings of Divine Power

Christ gave us the sacraments not as symbols but as **encounters with His living presence**.

The Eucharist — the source and summit

Every grace needed for holiness flows from the Eucharist.

Receiving Jesus strengthens patience, purifies desires, and renews courage.

Regular Mass attendance and Eucharistic Adoration are essential for anyone seeking to live their baptismal mission.

Confession — the sacrament of victory

Spiritual warfare is won in the confessional.

There we receive:

- forgiveness
- restoration
- freedom
- grace to resist temptation
- the humility that makes the devil flee

A monthly confession (or more frequent when needed) keeps the heart light and the conscience clear.

The other sacraments

- **Baptism** gives identity and authority.
- **Confirmation** equips us for mission through the Holy Spirit.
- **Marriage** and **Holy Orders** strengthen those called to lay down their lives for others.
- **Anointing of the Sick** brings healing and peace in suffering.

The sacraments are the armor of the Christian soldier.

III. The Reality of Spiritual Warfare

Spiritual warfare is not a dramatic myth.

It is the quiet, daily contest between grace and temptation, truth and deception, love and selfishness.

The enemy's strategy is subtle

The devil prefers whispers over explosions:

- discouragement
- resentment
- loneliness
- distractions
- hidden sins
- lies about identity
- fear of holiness

He seeks not to terrify but to wear down.

Christ's authority protects the baptized

We fight with Christ's victory, not our own strength.

A Christian remains safe when they remain:

- in a state of grace
- rooted in Scripture
- faithful in prayer
- accountable in community

The enemy cannot overcome the soul that clings to Jesus.

IV. Weapons for the Battle

1. Scripture

God's Word exposes lies and strengthens the heart.

Memorizing a few key verses becomes a shield in moments of temptation:

- "The Lord is my shepherd."
- "Be not afraid."
- "I can do all things in Christ."
- "Come to Me, all who are weary."

2. The Rosary

The Rosary is a chain that binds the enemy.

With each Hail Mary, we invite Our Lady to crush evil beneath her heel.

3. Sacramentals

Holy water, blessed medals, crucifixes, and the sign of the cross are real channels of grace.

They remind us that we belong to Christ.

4. Fasting

Fasting purifies desire, disciplines the will, and strengthens prayer.

5. Community

The Christian life is not a solo mission.

Isolation weakens; fellowship protects.

Even one trustworthy friend strengthens resistance.

V. Discernment: Hearing God's Voice in a Noisy World

Distinguishing God's voice from the enemy's

God speaks with:

- peace
- clarity
- humility
- encouragement toward virtue

The enemy speaks with:

- pressure
- confusion
- pride
- discouragement

When in doubt, bring the situation into the light of prayer, Scripture, and wise counsel.

Conscience as Christ's ambassador

A well-formed conscience becomes a powerful instrument of the kingly mission — guiding decisions, correcting faults, and prompting deeper holiness.

VI. Perseverance: The Mark of the Mature Disciple

The Christian's greatest victories are often unseen:

- resisting a temptation
- forgiving a wound
- persevering in prayer when tired
- choosing kindness when annoyed
- remaining faithful in trials

Spiritual maturity is measured not by dramatic moments but by daily fidelity.

Reflection Questions

1. What prayer habit do I need to strengthen or restore?
2. When was my last good confession?
3. Which spiritual weapon am I being invited to use more intentionally?

Closing Prayer

*Lord Jesus Christ, Victor over sin and death,
draw me close to Your Sacred Heart.*

Strengthen me through prayer, nourish me with Your Eucharistic Presence, heal me through Your mercy in Confession, and guard me from every deception of the enemy.

Clothe me with Your light and guide my steps in the way of holiness, so that I may live my baptismal mission with courage and joy. **Amen.**

CHAPTER 12

The Works of Mercy

Introduction — Love Made Visible

The Christian life is inseparable from concrete acts of love.

Christ did not simply teach about mercy — He embodied it:

- touching lepers,
- feeding the hungry,
- forgiving sinners,
- comforting the broken,
- raising the dead,
- and laying down His life for all.

To follow Jesus is to love as He loves.

The works of mercy are the practical, everyday pathways by which the baptized participate in His priestly, prophetic, and kingly mission.

Mercy **evangelizes, heals, transforms,** and **reveals Christ's Heart** to a hurting world.

I. Mercy as the Heart of Mission

Pope Benedict XVI once said:

> "Being Christian is not the result of an ethical choice, but the encounter with a Person."

Works of mercy extend that encounter to others.

Mercy is not an optional extra; it is the living expression of baptismal identity. When the world sees Christians feeding the hungry, visiting the sick, comforting the sorrowing, and forgiving offenses, it sees the Gospel embodied.

Mercy is the Church's most persuasive apologetic.

II. The Scriptural Mandate

Jesus identifies Himself with the most vulnerable:

> "I was hungry and you gave Me food…
> I was a stranger and you welcomed Me…
> Whatever you did for one of the least of these,
> you did it to Me."
> — Matthew 25:35–40

These words are not poetry.

They are judgment.

They are promise.

They are mission.

Christ hides behind the faces of the poor so that love becomes personal, not theoretical.

III. The Corporal Works of Mercy

The corporal works of mercy address the physical needs of the body — the places where human dignity is most visibly wounded.

1. Feed the Hungry

Hunger wounds the image of God.

Every meal offered becomes an act of Eucharistic imitation, reflecting Christ who feeds His people with His own Body.

Practical steps:

- Bring meals to a struggling family
- Volunteer at a soup kitchen
- Keep snacks or care bags in your car

2. Give Drink to the Thirsty

This includes not only water but access to clean drinking resources, compassion for addiction struggles, and kindness toward anyone spiritually "dry."

3. Clothe the Naked

Clothing offers dignity.

It also reminds us of Adam and Eve's first experience of shame — and God's tender response.

4. Shelter the Homeless

A Christian home should be a place of refuge.

Hospitality is one of the most ancient forms of evangelization.

5. Visit the Sick and Imprisoned

Presence is powerful.

A short visit often does more good than long speeches.

In prisons and hospitals, despair is real — so grace must be present.

6. Bury the Dead

To bury the dead is to proclaim the resurrection.

It treats the human body with reverence, affirming that death does not have the final word.

IV. The Spiritual Works of Mercy

Where the corporal works heal the body, the spiritual works heal the soul — the deeper hunger of the human heart.

1. Instruct the Ignorant

Sharing the faith is an act of love, not superiority.

Parents especially are called to instruct their children patiently and clearly.

2. Counsel the Doubtful

Doubt is not sin; it is an invitation to guidance.

A listening ear and a hopeful word can rescue a soul from despair.

3. Admonish the Sinner

Done with humility, this is a rescue mission, not a condemnation.

It seeks the eternal good of the other.

4. Comfort the Sorrowful

Suffering must never be faced alone.

A Christian presence becomes the tenderness of Christ.

5. Forgive Offenses

Every act of forgiveness repeats the Cross.

Forgiveness is the most powerful spiritual work of mercy because it shatters the devil's grip.

6. Bear Wrongs Patiently

Patience under injustice is a silent imitation of Christ.

It purifies the heart and strengthens the will.

7. Pray for the Living and the Dead

Prayer unites the whole Mystical Body — earth, purgatory, and heaven.

Intercessory prayer is one of the Christian's greatest privileges.

V. Mercy as Evangelization

Many people will accept food or comfort long before they accept doctrine.

Mercy opens the heart so truth can enter.

The early Church grew not through programs but through **radical charity**:

- rescuing abandoned infants,
- tending to the dying during plagues,
- feeding widows and orphans,
- freeing slaves,
- comforting the persecuted.

People were converted because Christian love was unmistakable.

The world may debate theology, but it cannot deny sacrificial love.

VI. Integrating Mercy into Daily Life

Mercy does not always require large commitments.

Small habits form a lifestyle of compassion:

- Slow down and listen

- Offer a sincere compliment
- Hold the door for someone struggling
- Send a note of encouragement
- Notice the lonely
- Share a meal with someone who needs company
- Let someone go ahead of you in line

The smallest act, when done with love, becomes a conduit of grace.

VII. A Family Culture of Mercy

Parents teach mercy best by example.

A family grows in holiness when:

- siblings forgive each other
- meals are shared joyfully
- the poor are remembered
- elderly relatives are visited
- prayer is interwoven into daily life

Children raised in mercy become adults capable of great compassion.

VIII. Mercy's Double Transformation

Mercy changes the recipient —
but it also changes the giver.

Serving the poor reveals our own poverty.

Forgiving others reveals our own wounds.

Comforting the suffering strengthens our compassion.

Loving those who struggle softens our pride.

Every act of mercy draws us nearer to the Heart of Christ.

Reflection Questions

1. Which corporal or spiritual works of mercy is God inviting me to practice more intentionally?
2. How can I integrate small acts of mercy into my daily routines?
3. Who in my family, parish, or workplace needs a gesture of mercy from me this week?

Closing Prayer

Lord Jesus,
You are Mercy incarnate.
Open my eyes to see You
in the hungry, the lonely, the sick, and the forgotten.

Make my heart generous,
my hands ready,
and my life a witness to Your compassion.

May every act of mercy I offer
draw others — and myself — closer to Your Sacred Heart.

Amen.

CHAPTER 13

Testimony, Witness & Evangelization

Introduction — Evangelization Begins in the Heart

Evangelization is not first a strategy, nor a program, nor a task assigned to "experts."

It begins with **a heart transformed by Christ.**

When the baptized encounter the love of God — truly, personally, deeply — something awakens within them that cannot remain silent. Grace seeks expression. Joy seeks witness. Love seeks to be shared.

Evangelization is simply **the overflow of a life touched by God.**

As Archbishop Fulton Sheen so often reminded the faithful:

"Our duty is not so much to win arguments, but to radiate Christ."

This chapter explores how personal testimony, daily witness, and courageous love can become a living proclamation of the Gospel — in homes, workplaces, parishes, and ordinary encounters.

I. The Nature of Christian Witness

1. Witness Flows from Encounter

The apostles did not begin evangelization with a textbook.

They began with an encounter — **"We have seen the Lord"** (John 20:25).

Likewise, your faith story is the foundation of your missionary life:

- How Christ found you
- How grace transformed you
- How the sacraments sustain you
- How God continues to shape your daily life

Your lived relationship with Jesus is your first and most powerful witness.

2. Witness is a Way of Life

Holiness is the most compelling apologetic.

Joy, patience, forgiveness, honesty, courage — these virtues preach louder than words.

A Christian who loves deeply, suffers faithfully, and serves generously becomes a living homily.

3. Witness is Accessible to Everyone

Some preach in pulpits; others preach by how they work, drive, parent, forgive, and bless.

Your life has a mission field uniquely shaped by God:

- your marriage,
- your family,
- your office,
- your friendships,
- your neighborhood,
- your gifts and limitations.

Evangelization begins right where you stand.

II. Sharing Your Testimony

Your personal testimony is one of the most powerful tools for evangelization — not because of eloquence, but because **your story is real**.

1. Center the Story on Christ

A testimony is not an autobiography.

It is a proclamation of what God has done:

- moments of grace
- times of forgiveness
- breakthroughs in prayer

- quiet perseverance in suffering

It answers the simple but profound question:

"How has Jesus Christ changed my life?"

2. Simplicity and Humility

People are moved by authenticity, not polish.

Speak plainly.

Speak gratefully.

Speak with humility about struggles, victories, and ongoing conversion.

3. Tailored to the Listener

A coworker may only need two minutes of hope.

A retreat group may welcome a deeper reflection.

A friend in crisis may be ready for an invitation to pray.

Discernment is itself an act of love.

4. Testimony Opens Doors

Your story often awakens questions:

- "How did you find peace through that trial?"
- "Where did you learn to pray like that?"
- "What helped you return to the Church?"

This is where evangelization begins: one curious heart at a time.

III. Evangelization Through Presence, Friendship & Conversation

1. Presence Before Proclamation

People must first encounter Christ's presence in you before they will listen to Christ's words from you.

Presence means:

- undivided attention
- genuine interest
- patient listening
- seeing Christ in each person

In a distracted world, such presence is a rare gift.

2. Friendship as a Channel of Grace

The Gospel usually travels at the speed of relationship.

Jesus evangelized through friendship —
sharing meals, walking dusty roads, asking questions, listening deeply.

When trust grows, conversations about faith unfold naturally.

3. The Power of Ordinary Moments

Evangelization happens in:

- the grocery aisle
- the hospital waiting room

- the break room at work
- the hockey rink
- the back porch at dusk

Grace loves the ordinary.

4. Speaking with Gentleness and Courage

Evangelization does not impose; it proposes.

But proposal requires courage:

the courage to speak a kind word, offer to pray, or gently share a Scripture passage.

IV. Evangelization Through Charity & Sacrifice

Words alone cannot bear the Gospel's weight.

Love must take flesh.

1. The Works of Mercy as Evangelization

When Christians:

- feed the hungry,
- visit the sick,
- forgive offenses,
- console the sorrowful,
- shelter the homeless,
  they preach Christ more convincingly than any argument.

2. Sacrifice as a Witness of Love

When you suffer patiently, forgive deeply, or serve quietly, others see a strength not your own.

The Cross is the great evangelizer.

V. Offering Invitations to Christ and the Church

Evangelization eventually calls for invitation:
to prayer, to Mass, to reconciliation, to community.

1. Invitation with Freedom

Never coercion — only love.

A gentle, joyful invitation allows the Holy Spirit room to work.

2. Accompaniment

Offer to:

- sit with them at Mass,
- meet for coffee afterward,
- answer questions,
- walk the journey with them.

3. Community Matters

A vibrant parish or small group becomes a home where seekers discover belonging, joy, and healing.

VI. Overcoming Fear, Apathy, and Discouragement

Fear whispers, "You may offend."

Apathy murmurs, "Someone else will do it."

Discouragement sighs, "It won't make a difference."

1. Courage from the Holy Spirit

The apostles hid in fear until Pentecost.

Then they became fearless.

That same Spirit lives in you.

2. Small Steps Build Boldness

Begin with simple acts:

- mention a Sunday homily
- offer to pray for someone
- share a saint's quote
- speak of how God helped you today

Courage grows by use.

3. Trust God with the Results

Your task: **witness.**

God's task: **conversion.**

Do your part with love and peace.

Reflection Questions

1. What part of my own spiritual story is God inviting me to share more freely?
2. Where in my daily life is the Holy Spirit prompting me to be more courageous in witness?
3. Which relationships in my life may be ready for a deeper spiritual conversation or invitation?

Closing Prayer

Holy Spirit,
You filled the apostles with courage and joy.
Fill my heart with the same fire.

Give me the words to speak,
the patience to listen,
the charity to love,
and the courage to witness to Christ
in every place You send me.

Make my life a living testimony,
so that others may see Your goodness
and seek Your face.

Amen.

CHAPTER 14

The Christian Life as a Missionary Journey

Introduction — A Pilgrimage of Love

The Christian life is not static; it is a journey.

It begins at baptism, deepens through the sacraments, matures through trials, and blossoms in loving service.

Every baptized person walks a missionary path — not necessarily across oceans, but across living rooms, office hallways, parish parking lots, and grocery store aisles. The Lord leads us step by step, inviting us to become saints in the very circumstances we inhabit.

> "Life is a journey, not a destination —
> and Christ walks with us every step."
> — Archbishop Fulton J. Sheen

Mission is not an activity we "add" to life; it *is* the Christian life, lived with a heart open to God's voice and the needs of others.

I. Baptism: The Beginning of the Journey

Every missionary journey begins at the font.

In baptism:

- we are claimed by Christ,
- anointed as priest, prophet, and king,
- and sent forth into the world as His partners in love.

This identity is not symbolic — it is *ontological*.

Something in us has been changed forever.

Baptism plants the seeds of mission; the rest of life is the unfolding of that grace.

A Daily Return to Baptism

The baptized disciple:

- remembers the call,
- renews it through prayer and sacrament,
- and rediscovers each day what it means to belong to Christ.

Missionary life begins not with doing, but with **being His**.

II. A Journey Shaped by the Threefold Mission of Christ

Every Christian walks with Jesus as:

- **Priest** (offering daily life as sacrifice),
- **Prophet** (speaking truth with love),

- **King** (leading through service and mastery of self).

These three dimensions shape the missionary journey in every season of life.

1. The Priestly Path

The Christian learns to offer:

- joys,
- sorrows,
- fatigue,
- work,
- relationships

as a living sacrifice united to the Eucharist.

This transforms ordinary life into holy ground.

2. The Prophetic Path

The prophet listens before speaking.

He studies God's Word, prays with Scripture, and responds with a heart rooted in love.

The prophetic role is exercised in:

- teaching children
- encouraging a struggling friend
- bearing witness to truth in the workplace
- offering spiritual counsel

- defending the dignity of human life in quiet, courageous ways

3. The Kingly Path

The kingly mission begins with mastery of self:

- choosing virtue,
- practicing discipline,
- ordering desires toward God.

From this inner throne flows outward service — guiding one's home, parish, and community with humility and justice.

III. The Stages of the Missionary Journey

The missionary life unfolds like a pilgrimage, with seasons of:

- learning,
- struggle,
- growth,
- surrender,
- and fruitfulness.

1. Encounter

Every journey begins with an encounter with Christ — sometimes dramatic, often gentle.

This encounter awakens love, conversion, and desire.

2. Formation

The disciple is then formed by:

- Scripture
- Sacraments
- Spiritual reading
- Mentorship
- Community

Formation equips the heart for service.

3. Mission

Formation leads naturally to mission.

The disciple begins to share what he has received:

- in friendship
- in family life
- in acts of mercy
- in evangelization
- in witness

4. Perseverance

Every mission faces resistance — both from without and within.

Dryness, setbacks, misunderstandings, and trials purify love.

Perseverance is one of the strongest forms of evangelization.

5. Fruitfulness

Eventually the seed planted through witness bears fruit — sometimes seen, often unseen.

Missionary fruitfulness belongs to God; our part is fidelity.

IV. Walking the Daily Path with Christ

The missionary journey is sustained by simple, consistent habits:

1. Daily Prayer

Five or ten minutes of quiet each day reorders the heart.

Prayer keeps the missionary grounded, peaceful, and attentive to God's voice.

2. Frequent Sacraments

The Eucharist strengthens; Reconciliation renews.

These sacraments restore the missionary heart and supply divine strength where human strength fails.

3. Scripture as a Companion

Reading even a small portion of Scripture each day shapes the mind of Christ within the disciple.

4. Community Support

No missionary walks alone.

Shared prayer, fellowship, and encouragement lighten the burden and multiply the joy.

V. A Mission Marked by Love, Joy, and Hope

1. Love as the Mark of a Missionary

The Christian is known not by brilliance but by charity.

Love is the signature of Christ in the world.

2. Joy as a Sign of God's Presence

True joy is not superficial cheerfulness; it is the deep gladness that flows from belonging to God.

A joyful Christian is a living invitation to faith.

3. Hope in Every Season

Missionaries walk with hope because they know Who walks with them.

Even trials become opportunities to proclaim God's faithfulness.

> **"Faith tells us that Christ walks the roads of life with us, even when we do not recognize Him."**
> — Archbishop Fulton J. Sheen

Reflection Questions

1. Which part of the missionary journey am I living most intensely right now — encounter, formation, mission, perseverance, or fruitfulness?

2. How can I root my daily routines more deeply in prayer and sacrament?

3. Where might the Holy Spirit be calling me to take a simple step of love, courage, or witness this week?

Closing Prayer

Lord Jesus,
You walked the roads of Galilee and Judea,
and You walk with me now.

Guide my steps on this missionary journey.
Strengthen me in prayer,
sustain me in trial,
fill me with Your joy,
and lead me to love with Your own Heart.

Make my life a living proclamation of Your Kingdom
until I reach the heavenly home You prepare for all Your children.

Amen.

EPILOGUE

A Lifestyle of Missionary Joy

The Christian life is far more than a set of obligations or a list of religious practices.

It is an adventure of love — a daily walk with Christ that gradually transforms the heart and radiates outward to the world.

Every baptized believer carries a mission written into the soul by God Himself.

The more deeply we receive His love, the more naturally we share it.
When Christ dwells within us, joy becomes the overflow of His presence.

"Joy is the infallible sign of the presence of God."
— Archbishop Fulton J. Sheen

This joy is not naïve optimism.

It is the confidence that Christ is alive, active, and victorious — even in a world marked by confusion and suffering.

A joyful Christian is a living contradiction to despair, a quiet sign that the Kingdom has already begun.

The Everyday Places Where Mission Happens

Missionary joy unfolds in simple, ordinary moments:

- a kind word at the supermarket,
- patience with a difficult coworker,
- forgiveness offered to a family member,
- a prayer spoken for someone in distress,
- a generous act done in secret.

These small gestures become mighty seeds of grace.

The world hungers not for arguments but for love that looks like Christ.

Wherever you stand — home, parish, workplace, digital space — you stand on missionary ground.

A Heart Rooted in Prayer

Joyful mission is sustained by a living friendship with God.

Prayer is the wellspring where the missionary heart finds:

- clarity,
- strength,
- healing,
- courage,
- and deep peace.

Frequent encounters with Christ in the Eucharist and in Confession renew the soul.

In silence before the tabernacle, burdens lighten and zeal is rekindled.

Without prayer, mission becomes activism.

With prayer, mission becomes love.

A Community Strengthened Together

The missionary journey is never walked alone.

In the early Church, disciples gathered to pray, to break bread, to encourage one another, and then to go forth.

The same rhythm sustains missionary joy today.

When believers pray together, support one another, and share the joys and trials of discipleship, they become a living flame — a light that grows brighter as it is shared.

A joyful parish, a praying family, a faithful small group — these are the places where missionary fire is born and sustained.

Courage for the Road Ahead

The world needs your witness.

Not because you are perfect, but because Christ is perfect in you.

Not because you have all the answers, but because you carry the One who is the Answer.

There will be misunderstandings, challenges, and moments of discouragement.

Yet the Holy Spirit who strengthened the apostles strengthens you as well.

Trust Him.

Take small, faithful steps.

Love generously.

Let Christ shine through your life without fear.

He will do the rest.

A Prayer for Missionary Joy

Lord Jesus Christ,
fill my heart with the joy of Your presence.
Make me a vessel of Your love in every place You send me.
Teach me to see each day as a mission,
each encounter as grace,
each difficulty as a chance to trust You more.

Strengthen me through prayer,
renew me through Your sacraments,
and unite me with fellow disciples
so that together we may bring Your light to the world.

Let my life be a quiet invitation to Your Heart,
until every soul knows the joy that comes from You alone.

Amen.

About the Author

ALLAN SMITH is a Catholic evangelist, radio host, and spiritual director who has spent over a decade proclaiming the wisdom of Archbishop Fulton J. Sheen to audiences worldwide. As the founder of Bishop Sheen Today, Al has edited and published dozens of classic Sheen titles, including 'The Cries of Jesus from the Cross' and 'Lord, Teach Us to Pray'.

A passionate promoter of Eucharistic Reparation and devotion to the Holy Face of Jesus, Al regularly speaks at parish missions, leads retreats, and hosts weekly radio broadcasts across Canada, the United States, Ireland, Australia and the Philippines. His work has helped reintroduce Sheen's powerful spiritual legacy to a new generation.

He lives in Canada with his family and continues his mission of calling souls to deeper intimacy with Christ through the example of saints like St. Thérèse of Lisieux and the timeless teachings of Fulton Sheen.

To learn more or to access free devotional resources, visit our two websites at:

www.bishopsheentoday.com

www.holyfacemiracle.com

A Personal Invitation

Over the years, I have had the privilege of helping souls draw closer to Christ through prayer, silence, and the beautiful wisdom of Archbishop Fulton J. Sheen.

If this devotional has nourished your heart, you may also find these works helpful in your journey of faith:

Advent and Christmas with Archbishop Fulton J. Sheen - *A Devotional Journey of Waiting, Welcoming, and Living the Mystery*

Daily readings and gentle reflections to guide the heart from hope to joy — from the quiet longing of Advent to the radiant wonder of Christmas.

The Holy Face and the Little Way - *A Spiritual Friendship with Christ, St. Thérèse, and the Holy Face*

A devotional for those seeking healing, confidence in God, and a deeper intimacy with Jesus in the quiet places of the soul.

Behold Your Mother - *Mary, the Cross, and the Power of Reparation*

A guide to loving Mary as Christ loves her, and to discovering the strength that comes from offering our lives in union with hers.

The Cross and the Last Words - *A Journey Through Calvary with Fulton J. Sheen*

Meditations for Lent, Holy Week, and every season in which the heart longs for mercy, meaning, and love that endures.

Lord, Show Us Thy Face, and We Shall Be Saved - *A Mission of Light, Truth, and Eucharistic Renewal*

A call to return to the Heart of Christ through Adoration, humility, and surrender.

The Sheen Mission Series — Collected Meditations

A treasury to keep on the nightstand — for those ten-minute moments of quiet that become encounters with God.

May these works draw you deeper into prayer, trust, and peace.

To learn more or to stay connected:
www.bishopsheentoday.com

www.ingramcontent.com/pod-product-compliance
Lightning Source LLC
Chambersburg PA
CBHW071302040426
42444CB00009B/1839